A DARK CLOUD
*And how to try to lift it from
the person you love*

Ty Harvey

© 2022 by Ty Harvey
ISBN 979-8-218-08968-9

INTRODUCTION

The author of this little book has been replaced by a bird, an authority on the subject covered in the following pages. There you'll find nine different rituals meant to lift a dark cloud from your lover, including explanations of why each should work. It's all meant to help those who've fallen for someone with a dark cloud over them and to prompt the reader to question their ideas of love, commitment, and how far one can rightly go to bring change in another's life.

It's also about birds, like me. Thanks for spending time with it.

CHAPTER ONE

Here a bird will explain how a dark cloud forms and what you might can do to change it. The bird will also show you how the most important parts of someone's life story are those that are hidden from them.

The person you love[1] has a dark cloud over them, and it seems like it'll never go away. That's why you're here, or it should be why, because trying your best to lift that dark cloud is what this little book is for.

But really, should you even be trying? No matter how much you love them, is this your business at all? Are you sure you're not focusing on their shortcomings to distract yourself from your own? Do you fantasize about being a hero, like that's the only way you'll ever deserve to be

---

[1] sex love

loved? You should probably answer these questions first before you keep moving forward here.

But maybe something recently happened to make you see just how dark and low their cloud is. Maybe now you feel personally challenged to fight it. Or maybe you got used to their dark cloud hovering over everything until one day you realized how sick of it all you are. Maybe your heart won't let you walk away, so fighting seems to be your only option. Either way, you're here, and this is to try to lift their dark cloud.

Now, before you can do anything to lift it, you need to accept that you might not be able to. In fact, it's probably impossible, but you shouldn't let this alone stop you. No matter how hopeless the endeavor is, some things are worth doing, and lifting their dark cloud might be one of those things since they're the person you love. That's why this book is about trying. So, from here on out, you'll find no mention of the impossibility of lifting the dark cloud. You should forget about this aspect and just try if you're going to try at all.

Next, you need to understand what the dark cloud is and what it isn't, and to do that, you'll need to see the person you love in a new way. So, invite them to your home, or if you already live together, ask them to set aside some time for you on a specific night.

—

When that night comes, if you can, let part of yourself become a little bird like me and follow the person you love all the way from wherever they are to your home. Watch how they walk. How they furrow their brow when they think. Once they arrive and you're both in the house, don't tell them anything about what you're doing. Just tell them you wanted to be with them, which is true. Listen to them. Love on them. Get them naked and lay with them as you ordinarily do.

While you run your fingers on their skin, look at them and think of everything you love about them. Think of every aspect of them that's free of that dark cloud. Their smile. The good ways they treat you. All the details that make them unique and special to you. Think of all the reasons you find them valuable enough to love them with their dark cloud.

Make a list in your head of everything good about the person you love. Ask yourself if they know that you love all these traits about them, if they know they have these qualities at all. Make note of whether they're aware of these things as you make your list. Try not to leave out a single feature you love about them. Look at how they make you love them. See the cycle of them being them and you being moved to give them love in all the ways you do. Know that your love is no secret to them.

Then, look at everything that makes up their dark cloud and accept that the cloud comes from them and only them. Don't make excuses for them. Maybe it's made up of their insecurities or anxiety or plain stupidity or drunkenness. Perhaps it's there because they're vindictive or easily offended. Maybe they have all of these traits and more because they're haunted by demons you can't see. Real demons with horns and tails and fangs. There's no way for you to know. All you can do is look at the parts of them that come together and create a fountain of bad living. Let the person you love be flawed. Let them be an imperfect human. Accept the possibility that they may be a loser.

Actively make a second list in your head of everything bad about the person you love. Ask yourself if they know the damage done by the way they are, if they know they have these qualities at all. Make note of whether they're aware of these things as you make your list. Try not to leave out a single unwanted feature they have. Look at how they make their life hard to live. See the cycle of them being them and the repercussions of their actions going outward and turning back on them. Know that their dark cloud is no secret to them.

Once you've looked at those two sides of them, the beautiful soul that brings goodness into their life and the flawed fool that creates endless problems for themself, now would be a good time to give them a kiss. Then, you need to recognize that there's something else there too. If you're going to act, recognize that there are things you need to learn and know or you'll have no chance against that dark cloud. And this is the first. Both you and the person you love need to see it.

So, tell them something like: "I read in a book the other day that everyone shares certain thoughts they think are only theirs, questions only asked by them, when in reality they're shared by everyone. It gave three questions and said that pretty much everyone has asked themselves at least one, and I want to see if you've ever asked yourself any of them."

Then, see if the person you love has ever wondered:

1. Are the colors you see the same as the colors others see?

2. Who in the past has had a crush on you or has been in love with you without you knowing?

3. Have you ever made a simple gesture or little mistake, like holding the door open for someone or turning without using your blinker, that was a part of a chain of events

that led to a horrible catastrophe you were completely unaware of?

Ask yourself these questions too and of course listen to the answers the person you love gives. Let them think and talk about whatever they choose, and as they do, realize that the reason the thoughts in these questions cross people's minds is that deep down everyone knows they can't actually see the world around them as it truly is. All people see is what's in their heads, while the actual stories of their lives reach far beyond what they can know. Let the person you love come to this understanding on their own if they do. Don't tell them.

Think about how everyone is affected by others while no one fully knows the ways others are affected by them. This makes up as much of one's story as anything. Consider the first person in history to jump on a horse and ride it. The first person to get in a boat and tell everyone goodbye and head out into the water to see what was there, accepting they may never return to their home. The impacts of those people's choices will resonate until the end of civilization.

Yet, they were human, and that means their head functioned much like yours no matter how courageous or crazy they were, filled with worry, distractions, hunger, thirst, boredom, horniness, the need for love, insecurity, wishes, and trivial ideas. You know nothing of those personal thoughts. All you can see is the impact their lives had on the world. They each changed the course of society forever in ways they never got to see and could never comprehend. That is their life story more than any thought they had.

The story of the person you love, although not as impactful on the world as the first boat explorer or the first person to ride a horse, is no different. Who has silently changed their course because of the person you love, inspired by them or in spite of them? Who's secretly hated them, jealous of things they achieved that the person you love didn't even consider valuable? Who's told stories of them, using them as the perfect example to make their point?

The answer to these questions makes up as much of their story if not more than their own view of their life. The unknown results of how they live, the effects that never come back, and the impact they have on the world around them that they will never know are the biggest parts of their story.

—

You also shouldn't forget that there's you, the person who loves them. You're here reading this hoping to help, but at the same time you're already a part of their story too, on multiple levels. The love you give drives them to do good things that bring goodness back to them, no doubt. And you feed that dark cloud, helping them make the wrong decisions and nurturing the lesser emotions that bring a bad life back on them, whether you want to admit it to yourself or not.

Then, there are the things you do out of love for them that never touch them, that just stay with you. Although they never know what happened, those moments add pretty little marks on their life. While the dark cloud is above, swirling with the effects of their foolish decisions and the demons that haunt them, and their own existence is beneath, lit by the brightness of their soul and the angels that try to save them, in between is how you're secretly moved by your love for them.

Others are moved by them too, of course, in ways never seen by them. Sometimes it's good. Sometimes it's bad, but either way the person you love never knows. It's this layer of their story, the secret layer that the person you love will never see, that you'll need to focus on to try to lift that dark cloud.

In the following chapters, you'll do exactly that. So, if you're finding yourself questioning whether you should be here, now's the time to stop. Maybe part of you is thinking you should walk away and just stay out of it. Maybe you don't think you have the energy, or maybe you feel like you'll just cause more problems. Maybe you don't think you're doing this for the right reasons, that you have a habit of giving too much to others and this is about to become just another one of those times. If you're starting to think this is a bad idea for you, that's fine. It's better to see that now than later. Take some time to think about it if you'd like. Go back to how things were and try to ignore what you've seen about the person you love if you need to. You can simply bookmark this page, and if you never come back, then you don't.

CHAPTER TWO

Here the bird will guide you through three rituals that join sexual intimacy, a dead fish, and a rag doll burned on a shoreline to urge fate to replace the worst qualities of the person you love. The bird will also show you how your hopes for others have a different power than the hopes you have for yourself.

On a beautiful warm day, again invite the person you love to be with you at your home, this time in the afternoon. Before they arrive, make the bed and straighten the bedroom and open the window and let the curtains blow in the breeze. While you do, think of all the things you hope for the person you love. Go ahead and start making a list in your head of every reasonable wish you could make for them. Meanwhile, look out the window and watch the birds. If you can, let part of yourself become a bird too. Fly back and forth between a tree and the window and think of the number of times in history people have wished they could fly.

Look at all your bird friends around you and how they live completely without wishes. Sure, birds have desires, but bird desires are for now, not a hope for later. Never once has a bird wished to someday become a human so they could sit on a couch, watch TV, and eat a hamburger. Birds don't think that way. We just want a hamburger if we see one and will swoop down and try to grab one off a picnic table if we get a chance or perch under your feet hoping someone drops a bit. Birds act on desire, perhaps fixate on it, and do all they can to get what they want, but birds don't wish.

Instead, birds watch humans. We've done it since the dawn of time. We watch people sow seed so we can come and eat it when they're gone. We sit perched on trash day to see if the garbage workers leave fallen scraps on the street. We watch people all the time, yet none of those people ever really notice, mainly because their heads are tied up with wishes. So, while humans are wishing, birds fill the space between the ground and the sky, watching the effects of people's actions and their dark clouds subsequently rise and fall. Every time someone has cried beside an open window. Every birthday party under the shade of a tree. Every time a child learned to ride a bike. Birds are everywhere circling and watching and listening to the lives of the humans around them unfold.

Realize all the things about humanity birds know. Then, ask yourself and the other birds around you, in the way birds do, something like: "Why do people make wishes? What makes humans think they can change anything at all just by declaring in their heads what they want?"

Listen as they tell you what any bird will tell you, that despite humans having no proof that wishing changes anything, doing so is an act all people share. Hoping somehow to make real the thoughts in their minds by invoking the generosity of a god or a spirit or another higher something that controls life. All people have done it. It's built into the idea of prayer in organized religions. It's the root of manifestation in other spiritual beliefs. And then, of course, there are birthday candles and falling stars. People make wishes because a part of them believes there's a chance a wish will come true if they wish it. Because sometimes wishes do come true. Skeptics would argue it's just a coincidence, but is it? There's no way for them to know. So, people keep on wishing. It's one of the things that makes people human.

But if you make a wish and it doesn't come true, is it a part of your story, or is it just another desire in the endless pile of desires in your head? The answer to this depends on who you're wishing for. If you make a wish for yourself and it doesn't come true, then it's just another thing you've wanted but didn't have. That list is practically infinite and worthless. But if you make a wish for someone else, that's different. Again, ask yourself how many people have wished they could fly since the dawn of humanity. Millions? Thousands are probably wishing it this very second. But how many people have wished someone else could fly? Has anyone ever wished that for another? Is anyone wishing that for someone else right now?

The human mind doesn't usually think like that. This is why being moved by the person you love enough to truly want something for them, going out of your way and actively asking fate to give them whatever you hope for them, undoubtedly leaves a pretty mark on their story. Like a love letter lost in the mail and never read, your wish, along with your intentions and effort, will be a part of their story even if your wish for them never comes true.

Yet, you want your wish to come true. That's the point. So, here you're going to do your best to change the life of the person you love in the way you believe they need. To do so, you're going to speak to the forces that control the world around us and present the specific changes you want for them. And to ensure you've done all you can, you'll try three different times in three different ways.

Each of the attempts are founded in the simplest manifestation ritual, the most basic elements shared by many cultures to make a wish come true—to write your wish on a piece of paper and then burn that paper to ashes. Of course, most renditions involve added astrology or incantations, but you won't be directed to do that here, although you're welcome to on your own. Instead, you will take the spirit of burning a list of wishes and make a greater effort. Three tries to make your wishes for your love come true. And your first try will be on this beautiful warm day.

Try #1

When the person you love arrives, don't rush them to the bedroom you straightened. Let them naturally find the freshly made bed by the open window. They'll lay on it and mess it up, as that's what you humans do. Once they do, lay there with them. Take off their clothes and yours and let the curtains move with your breathing.

For a moment, let part of yourself be a bird if you can. Perch outside your window and watch the two of you together. Meanwhile, resting beside them, ask the person you love about their day. Roll them on their belly and run your hands over their shoulders and back. While they talk, think of your list of wishes for them and think of what problem each wish would solve.

Choose a place on their body and, with your finger, write that problem on their skin. Then, with your finger, cross it out. Now, write your wish in its place. Choose another place on their body and write another problem on their skin. Cross it out and again write your wish in its place. Do this all over the body of the person you love. The backs of their legs. Their butt. Their ribs. Their scalp. The tops of their feet. Cover their body with X-ed-out problems overwritten by wishes.

When you've exhausted your list, roll them over and fuck them. While you do, imagine all those problems flowing out of their chest with every sigh or moan of your name, every breath out, until the spirit of every problem is gone. As they orgasm, imagine everything you hope for them flowing into them with each of their deep breaths in. As you lay together still, see them free of their problems with only your wishes for them remaining. When you're done, kiss them so deeply and gently, so full of love and tenderness, fate can't ignore you.

Try #2

For your second try, invite them to your home on a cold drizzly night. Before they arrive, buy a large whole fish from the grocery store and keep it hidden in the refrigerator. Have a nice dinner. Drink. Go to bed with them.

Once they're asleep, kiss them and get up from bed. Get dressed. Take the fish out of the refrigerator and, with a small knife, carve the worst traits of the person you love all along the fish's body. Carry the fish outside and find a spot to lay it, in the alley, behind your house, or beside a dumpster by a building. Set the fish there and find a comfortable place to watch from afar.

Wait there until a stray cat or raccoon or possum or fox or whatever comes for it. While you wait, remember the worst traits you scratched on the fish. Look up at the low-hanging clouds and how the streetlights illuminate them and watch for the shadow of a demon hovering over the fish. There could be one. Who knows. Wait as long as you must until something comes and takes that fish.

If you do see the shadow of a demon, watch it follow whatever animal carries the fish away. Know that you haven't gotten rid of that demon. It will keep coming back until the person you love makes it go away themselves.

Go home and go back to sleep. When you wake up, suggest you two go for a walk sometime that day. Once you go out, return to the place you left the fish. Stop and kiss them there by the dumpster or wherever. Hold them tightly and lick their neck. Taste the salt on their skin and smell the distinctive scent of your saliva mixed with them. Be so present with all of your senses in that moment that fate can't ignore you. Change your mind about the walk if you'd rather go home and take them back to bed.

Try #3
On a clear still night, make a large rag doll from old shirts or dish towels or whatever you have lying around. Name that doll Trouble. Use a

marker to write all the troubles of the person you love on the doll and then X them out.

Drive down to the nearest lake, wherever or however far it may be. Bring a lot of thick dry sticks, small twigs, and dry paper. Walk to the water's edge and find a nice place to sit.

Take a stick and run it through the rag doll and poke that stick deep enough in the mud for it to sturdily stand. Surround the doll with sticks and paper and twigs and light it all on fire. Make sure the entire rag doll burns and, while it does, watch the smoke of Trouble rise to the sky and dissipate. Leave the ashes on the shore.

The next day, invite the person you love on a picnic near the water. Make some sandwiches. Buy some wine. Then, take them to where you burned the rag doll named Trouble. While you eat sandwiches and drink wine, sit close to them and talk about the dreams you have together. Shoot off a few fireworks before you leave if you have some. At some point, you should kiss them and, as you do, put your hand on their throat as lightly or as tightly as you think they would like. Breathe to the pulse in their veins and feel the life running through their body. Feel it so clearly fate can't ignore you.

—

Once you've made these three tries, you're welcome to try more, like something with balloons or dynamite or an empty car speeding off a cliff, but really three is enough. No one would question whether you've made your best effort, and you have more to do anyway. But before you move on, see the space between your lover's beauty and the dark cloud above them widening. Believe what you've done has left pretty swollen marks on their story and has raised their dark cloud, even if just a bit.

If you find yourself questioning whether you should be doing so much for the person you love, push it out of your mind. What's making you do this? Do you subconsciously want to make them dependent on you so they'll never leave? Are you being obsessive for some other unclear or hidden reason? If you're asking yourself these questions, you either need to stop thinking that way or stop doing this entirely. To have a chance to lift that dark cloud, you have to simply do your best and let what happens be. Nothing more.

CHAPTER THREE

Here the bird will guide you through three rituals that join sacrifice, masturbation, and the sowing of wild-flower seed to do beautiful acts on behalf of the person you love. The bird will also show you how the use of your name beyond what you can see defines who you are without you knowing it.

One evening, make no plans with the person you love. Tell them you need time to yourself and reassure them that nothing is wrong between the two of you if they need such reassurance.

Then, go to the market and buy everything the person you love likes to eat. Get them a cake if they like cake. Steak if they like steak. Buy a whole slaughtered pig. Buy twenty pounds of Brussels sprouts and asparagus, ten bags of bar-becue potato chips. Whatever they love, get too much of it. Get a huge wreath of their favorite flowers. Get cases of bottles of their favorite drinks.

As you pick up each item, say to yourself the name of the person you love. Ask yourself how often their name has been spoken and watch that unknown number go up each time you say it. See their name attached to each item as you place it in your cart and wonder all the things their name has been attached to throughout their life. Perhaps their first bicycle, a favorite shirt, an item someone believes they stole but didn't, an item someone thinks the person you love stole because they did. Ask yourself to what things you attach the name of the person you love. Make a list in your head, every item, every topic, everything you connect with their name.

Meanwhile, as you walk through the grocery store, let part of yourself become a bird and fly up and sit on a light fixture hanging from the ceiling. Look out on all the shoppers as they move their way through the aisles and realize that everyone down there has a name, just like the person you love, and that someone is thinking about them too. Someone is most likely speaking the name of each person in the grocery store right now, but they don't know it. Someone could be lying about them or saying amazing things about them, but they can't feel it and its effect on their name because their name isn't actually a part of them.

Fly from person to person, perch above each of them for a moment, and listen to the things they say to themselves or whoever is with them when they think no one is listening. Watch the countless demons flow up and down the aisles following their people. Before you return to yourself, see how a little bird can take someone's name and fly around and fill the neighborhood with rumors.

The name of the person you love, along with everyone else's, was assigned to them by another, and the point of someone's name is to talk about them when they aren't around and to attach their name to things that others consider to be a part of them if they like it or not. Even if you don't want the name they gave you and change it to something that better suits you, the result is the same. Your name is for others to use, and you have no say in what they do with it.

Not only is your name used to refer to you and to attach it to things, but it can also be used to act on your behalf without you choosing or knowing. Someone can donate money in your name. Someone can take revenge in your name. Someone can win a game in your honor. Someone can dedicate a book to you and never tell you. Someone can climb any mountain, plant a flag in anyone's name, and forget to tell them once they get home. There are countless ways someone can be moved to do something in the name of someone else without ever letting them know.

If a life story is anything, it's what's attached to the person's name. And every time someone acts in that person's name and that person doesn't know about it, it leaves a positive or negative mark that lies between their self and their dark cloud. If it's a pretty act, it leaves a pretty mark, while ugly acts take pretty marks away. The bigger the gesture, the bigger the mark. The more lasting, more loving, the more focused the act, the better chance the mark will take up so much space it starts to lift that dark cloud.

So, here you're going to do your best to act in the name of the person you love in a way that is as big and pretty and focused and full of love as you can. Maybe you'll be able to lift that dark cloud a bit more. And to make sure you've done all you can, you'll try three different times in three different ways.

Try #1
When you get home from the grocery store, put everything away with care. Once you've done that, you need to choose an outdoor space where you'll have the most privacy, and where no one will mess with anything you put there. It can be your porch, your balcony, in the middle of a field, a hidden spot beside a dumpster, anywhere no one will care.

Once you've chosen your space, build a large altar there. Make it large enough to sacrifice a lamb or another living creature as they did in ancient times. If you can make it out of stone or brick, that would be best, but a table will do. Make sure to clean whatever you choose to use and leave no chairs around it.

Take all the food you bought for the person you love and cook any of it that needs to be cooked. Place on the altar the food, the flowers, the drink, everything else you got, and arrange it as neatly and beautifully as you can. Pour the drinks into nice glasses. Portion the food onto nice plates. Put out no silverware.

Once you've done all this, step back and look at the sky. Declare out loud to the universe something like: "If there's anything or anyone listening, if there's anything or anyone that looks over [insert the name of the person you love] and truly wishes them a good life, I sacrifice all of the things on this altar to you, in the name of [insert name of the person you love]."

Stand there and contemplate what sacrifice means. See that the difference between waste and sacrifice depends on where your energy, intentions, and heart lie. Think about how happy the person you love would be to see that you bought all of their favorite things. Notice that you've taken that happiness and have instead offered it to the powers that control their life.

And that's that. You can forget about it and go watch TV or do whatever you want. Let the birds eat the food you've left on the altar. Let the ants and mice and stray cats and possums and raccoons and anything else that wants it eat it. Watch the demons hover over the table wishing you had invited them too. Know they're not going away until the person you love gets rid of them.

Go to bed. Leave the food and drink there for as long as you can, days if possible, and then when nature has ruined it all, throw it away. Sacrifice it all, all the thought and energy and love you put into it, so much fate can't ignore you.

Try #2
Early in the morning, when the person you love is gone until tomorrow, let all your energy focus on your sexual attraction to them. Realize that every time you touch yourself with them in mind and without their knowledge, every time you touch yourself while imagining them touch-

ing you, you are acting in their name. And it's not just you. It applies to everyone who's fantasized about the person you love. Every lover, every crush, every stalker who has touched themselves with the person you love in mind. And how many times do you think that's happened? Who has imagined the person you love touching them, who has climaxed while completely consumed by thoughts of them, who more than anyone else? Is it you? Maybe.

But if it isn't you, who is it? It might be some unknown weirdo the person you love never met. What kind of marks did they leave on the life of the person you love? Were they loving marks? Degrading marks? There's no way to know unless you make sure that person is you. If it's you, you can leave no question to whether those marks are filled with genuine love and admiration and understanding. So, that's what you'll do.

Spend all day fantasizing with beautiful thoughts of the person you love while you touch yourself, dreaming it's them who's touching you. Let your brain swim in every idea about them that arouses you. Their scent, their essence. Their moles or freckles. Their physical presence. If their demons come to you, be prepared to embrace them with their horns and fangs because they may come, and right now you need to fully accept everything about your person.

For the moment, intertwine the brutal reality of your person and their demons with the sweet boundless sexuality you have for them and let the outcome speak for your love. Let your mind go to the darkest corners of intimacy with them until every idea fathomable, no matter how perverted or vulgar, has been explored and filled with love while you orgasm with their name on your lips. Let the demons cum too. Let them devour you if they want. Don't forget that they're not your demons and that no one can get rid of them but the person you love because they're a part of them. Show the demons that your love is bigger than all of their haunting combined.

Don't stop. Eat in bed while you do it or play with yourself in the kitchen with the refrigerator door open. Cum as many times as you can, your mind and body wholly tied to the person you love for the entire day and night until morning. Try to reach a thousand orgasms. Set an unreachable goal and do everything you can to achieve it. Make sure you'll forever hold the record for coming with them in mind, the most in a single day, an expression of love so clear that fate can't ignore you.

Try #3

Find a store that sells big bags of wildflower seeds and buy a bag or two. On your way home, think of every stranger, every group, and every organization that causes problems for the person you love. Consider all the places connected to those people and which of those places you and the person you love have never been to. If the person you love has legal trouble, think of all the jails and police stations and prisons you've never been to. If the person you love feels racially oppressed, think of all the neighborhoods those racists live in that you've never seen. A gang of robbers? What neighborhood are they from? Problems at work? Where is the corporate headquarters? A religious cult? Do they have a compound where they all live? Are any of these places nearby? Make a mental map of your city of all the unseen places home to those who cause problems for the person you love.

One morning, get up early with that map in your head and take those wildflower seeds with you in an unnoticeable bag. Visit every place on your map and discreetly drop wildflower seeds wherever you think flowers might grow. In the flower beds of the bank. In the strip of grass in front of the police station. Along the sidewalks of neighborhoods. Everywhere on the map.

Once you're done, go home. Or don't even go home. Go anywhere. It doesn't matter. All you need to do is move on because the point from here is to never go back if you can help it. Never go back to see if the wildflowers grew. The seeds may rot in the rain, be eaten by birds like me, blow away, refuse to germinate because you sowed them at the wrong time, or everywhere you tossed them could erupt in a bloom of beauty every year forever. A seasonal spectacle celebrated by everyone who sees it.

The same people who cause problems for the person you love may be the ones who walk by, filled with joy at the sight of all the flowers you sowed. If they do, that's okay. Let the flowers bring joy to everyone if they bloom at all. Be open to letting even those who don't deserve happiness from your labor have some. Be so open to the idea that fate can't ignore you.

—

Once you have made these three tries, you're welcome to try more, like things that involve climbing huge commercial radio towers or throwing a parade of mimes and miniature ponies, but really three should be enough. No one would question whether you've made your best effort, and you have more to do anyway. But before you move on, see the space between your lover's beauty and the dark cloud above them widening even greater. Believe what you've done has left a pretty swollen mark on their life and has raised the dark cloud even more.

CHAPTER FOUR

Here the bird will guide you through three rituals that join the bottom of a lake, the inside of a wall, and a high spot overlooking the city by creating monuments to the person you love. The bird will also show you how lasting relics of long-ago love are hidden around you.

Get up one day and go for a walk near your home in search of a big flat rock. This rock should be as big as you can comfortably carry and soft enough to deeply scratch with a nail if you try. Don't rush to find this rock. Find the perfect one. Take days if you have to.

While you search for this rock, ask yourself what you'd like on your tombstone. Everyone gets a monument to their death, and if you really wanted, you could dictate to others in your will what you'd like it to say. Instead of simply being a monument to you from the living, you could turn yours into a message from beyond death and say all kinds of things. Everyone could, but no one does because that's not what monuments are for. If you think of all the monuments, big and small, for the dead or the living, they are an expression by someone moved by whoever the monument is for. Monuments for soldiers are made by those who want their sacrifice to never be forgotten. Monuments for those who've died in catastrophes are made by their families or those touched by their stories. When a monument is created, someone hopes to capture and make permanent how they've been moved and to do so in a permanent and immovable way, so permanent and immovable, it creates a place. Because, in the end, a monument is a place.

Not only are there countless memorials to the dead, but there are also as many little monuments to love, joy, and celebration. They're everywhere old things still stand. Hearts carved in trees and in the seats of aged auditoriums and etched in cement sidewalks. Stones stacked by ancient humans to mark where momentous events occurred and carved with pictographs to commemorate achievements. Every monument is made by people to ensure the impact another has had on them isn't lost. And although someone else will most likely choose what is said on your tomb, you can choose to create your own monument for the person you love.

Unlike the other ways you've tried to lift that dark cloud, creating a monument is different. While manifesting and acting in their name create effects that go outward into the universe, they are fleeting moments of expressing your love. Meanwhile, a monument is tangible and permanent. The monument itself is a mark, constantly reverberating, constantly present, possibly forever, and there's probably no more effective way to leave a bigger, more beautiful mark on someone's story. So, that's what you're going to do. And to make sure you've done all you can, you will make three monuments in three different ways.

Try #1

Take home the stone and lay it on a table. Clean all the dirt and debris from it with soap and water and let it dry. Take a nail or other sharp object and scratch the name of the person you love into the stone. Scratch it deeply, tracing the letters over and over. Do it for hours. Think of the person you love as you do. Scratch a heart on there too, or a hundred. Go nuts if you want and keep it hidden from the person you love.

The next day, you need to find something that floats well enough that, if you place that stone on it in water, it won't sink. An inner tube would be good if you have one. A styrofoam lid might work if it's big enough. You could try making a raft by lashing small logs together with rope. Whatever it is, make sure it holds that stone on its own while floating on water. Even better, make sure it'll keep you afloat too.

Later that night, take your stone and your float to the closest lake. Put on some clothes you can safely swim in and take that stone and float out into the water. Swim behind the float and push it far into the middle. As you do, pay no mind to the demons that circle you. Ignore any thoughts of drowning, of a monstrous fish coming up for you from the deep and pulling you under by one of your legs, any thought a demon can make you have.

Turn back around and look at the shore from where you came. Look at the stars. Look at the silhouettes of the trees. Figure out exactly where you are in the lake. For a moment, let yourself be a bird like me, flying high above to see the spot where you swim. Look for markers and references so that if you ever choose to, you could point the spot out from the shore. Once you've done all this, yell out across the water that you love the person you love, push the stone off the float, and let it sink to the bottom of the lake. If demons are there, feel them sink with it but remember they'll always come back until the person you love gets rid of them.

Swim back to the shore using the float. Take your time and, when you get back, look out on the water and mark the place in the lake in your head where you let the stone drop. Do away with your float. Go home and shower. Hold the person you love while envisioning the place in the lake in your mind. See the stars. See the moon's reflection on the surface. See yourself floating there, one of thousands of creatures in a vast expanse of water.

Sometime in the next few days, invite the person you love to take a walk with you down by the lake. Stand with them where you entered and exited the water that night and kiss them. As you both stare out at the water's surface, ask them if they've ever wondered about all the things that have sunk to the bottom to never be seen again. As they answer, cling to them and take one of their hands and study their fingers in the moonlight as they talk. Kiss each knuckle with its own individual affection, one by one with an attentiveness fate can't ignore.

Try #2

Get a small wooden box. The smaller, the better. Go around the house and find every hair you can that's come from the body of the person you love. Pick hairs off their pillow, off their dirty clothes, off their razor. Pull a thread from their favorite piece of clothing. Take a coin from their pocket. Find a sheet of paper they've written on and tear a word from the paper, any word you choose. If you have to steal that paper from them, then do that, and put all these things in your little wooden box.

Go to your bed and move it away from the wall. Take a kitchen knife and cut a small hole in the wall directly where your heads lay together in bed when you kiss. Put the wooden box in the hole and, as you do, say to yourself everything you love about waking up beside them. Then, mend the wall and paint it the best you can so it looks no different from before. Or just fill it with so many wads of paper or something that no one will find the box there. Move the bed back where it goes.

When the person you love arrives, take them to the bedroom and undress them. If demons come, don't let them cause a fight between you. Be understanding if they're late. Respond gently if they're grumpy. Avoid meaningless quarrels about nothing because that's what demons will try to make you do. Think of the thread in the box as you pull off their clothes. Touch their hair. Play with their hands. Soak up their words.

And as you lay there together, take out a long ribbon and give them a pair of scissors. Hold each end of that ribbon in different hands and tell them to cut it. Don't let them ask any questions and, as soon as they cut it, kiss them and throw your body on theirs to erase the subject from their mind. Tie each of their wrists to the bedposts if they'd like that. Tie their ankles to the bed too. Blindfold them. Gag them. Lovingly conquer them with your ribbon, leaving them under your complete control. While you give yourself passionately to them as a moment of commemoration, feel the place you've created surrounding the bed and the two of you. See the box being there for as long as that building stands. Envision the couples who will put their beds there and lay together at the monument to your love. Tug on the ribbons that bind your person, knowing that the creation of a new place dedicated solely to love is something fate could never ignore.

Try #3

Get up early and dress for a hike. Get a map of your city and find the highest peak in the area, a beautiful overlook of where you live. Make sure it's part of a park or green space or some other land protected for generations to come. Go there and hike to this highest peak. While you do, start picking up stones the size of your fist, or your heart, and putting them in your bag that you're carrying. You're going to need at least a hundred of them, so you might as well start now.

When you get to the top, look out over where you live. Make out every place you can see that you know your person has been. Figure out the direction of where they are now and face them if you can. Either way, don't lose sense of which direction they are in.

Find a secluded place among the trees there at the top. Keep picking up stones and start placing them in a pile there. Once you have a hundred, choose a nice flat open spot between the trees and rake it clean with your feet. Now, place each stone on the earth, one touching the next, until you've made a big stone heart. Cover the stones with leaves so no one can see them.

Become a bird if you can and swoop down with the others to pick at the disturbed ground where your heart now lies. Then, perch yourself on a limb, look down at your heart, and see how the stones will slowly sink into the earth and remain there forever, as long as the area stays wild. Mark the spot of the heart in your mind and, as you set out to return home, leave your real heart there with the stone heart you made. For a little while, let yourself know what it feels like not to have your heart with you.

On a beautiful day soon after, invite the person you love on a hike. Take them where you left your heart. Feel your person's demons following you as you hike to the top. Hold the hand of the person you love as you look out over the city and point out places you've been together. Walk them inside the stone heart you built and kiss them there.

Now that you have your heart back and you're standing there with your person, ask yourself if you still truly love them. Are they really your person? After all you've done, all the love you've given without them knowing, do you still want to be with them? Or do you want to be done? If you'd rather not do this anymore, that's fine. You definitely need to accept you don't love them if you don't. It's okay to stop now and start acting awkward and get in a fight in the car on the way home the way people who've lost their love do.

But if you love them while standing in your heart made of stone, you'll know. Sure, demons might be circling you, but you're standing in a stone heart with the person you love that you made just for them. If there were ever a time and place where neither of your demons mattered, it's here and now. So, if you love them, turn your conversations to the future. Ask the person you love what they think life will be like in a hundred years. Ask them what they think will happen to the place where you're standing. If they say something that would destroy the heart you built, tell them that you hope not and hug them.

As the two of you leave to go back down the mountain, look back one last time and see the two of you inside that heart together. Imagine a part of you both staying there for eternity. Hope for it with a hope so pure and naive and blindly faithful fate can't ignore you.

—

Once you've done all these things, you could try more; it's true. And by now you should be able to come up with plenty of ways on your own to lift that dark cloud. If there's anything you really want to do, then do it. Otherwise, all the things you've done should be enough. No one would question whether you've made your best effort, and sooner or later, you have to move on and see what happens. So, one last time, envision the space between the beautiful things of your lover and the dark cloud above them widening. Believe the things you've done have been enough to lift that dark cloud far above the person you love.

Then, accept that it's time to forget. For any of the things you've done here to work, the person you love must never know, and that means you need to forget it all like it never happened so there's no chance you'll slip up and tell them one day. Because—be honest with yourself—if you keep remembering, if you keep waiting and watching to see the results of your actions, you're going to either accidentally mention what you've done or keep subconsciously trying to lift their dark cloud until the person you love begins to sense something isn't right. Both of those outcomes will keep the results of your actions from following their natural course and will negate all of your work.

So, make sure your beautiful acts of love for them go out into the world and never return to them. And to do that, just forget. Forget everything in this book. Push out of your mind any thought of how proud you are to have done all the things here, how much they should appreciate you and your love, or how you hope you've lifted their dark cloud.

CHAPTER FIVE

*Here the bird will teach you a game for forgetting. It
will also show you the relationship between the house
sparrow and humankind.*

On a rainy day, invite the person you love to
spend time with you yet again. Straighten your
living room and turn off everything that makes a
sound, every distraction. When they arrive, sit
close and amorously with them and tell them
you want to play a game. Tell them you read in a
book somewhere that you can intentionally forget memories and that the book had a game to
help. Then, to play the game, do the following:

1. Get a piece of paper and a pen for each of you
and sit across the table from each other. Both of
you are to think of ten frequent memories that

you'd like to forget. Don't write those memories down.

2. Instead, think of a simple item or action that evokes each memory you want to forget. Write down the item or action associated with each memory. (For instance, if you want to forget that you saw your uncle stabbed, write down *knife* if knives often evoke that memory. If you were pushed around by a bully in elementary school and you haven't enjoyed playgrounds since, write down *playground*. If someone was touching your ear at the moment a car you were once riding in collided with a tree, write down *someone touching your ear*.)

3. Now, beside each of those ten entries, write down a new thing you'd like to associate with that entry, something you want, something you could have in your future if you simply tried and did it, something to replace what you'd like to forget. (So, beside *knife*, write something else that you could associate it with, such as having a perfectly cooked steak, or if you want to be cute, you can connect it to something sexual with the

54

person you love, using a knife to strip them naked, cutting their clothes from their body. For *playground*, you could connect it to one of the longest slides in the world, or you could decide to sneak into a real playground at night and get drunk with the person you love and actually have some fun on a playground for once. Or you could write down the idea of putting a swing in your bedroom. Beside *someone touching your ear,* you could write the person you love kissing you on a rollercoaster with their hand on your cheek and touching your ear, or something like that.)

Either way, make a pair for all ten. It should look like this:

knife	*steak*
playground	*bedroom swing*
ear touched	*kissed on a rollercoaster*

XXXXXXXXXXXXX   XXXXXXXXXXXXX

XXXXXXXXXXXXX   XXXXXXXXXXXXX

XXXXXXXXXXXXX   XXXXXXXXXXXXX

XXXXXXXXXXXXX   XXXXXXXXXXXXX

XXXXXXXXXXXXX   XXXXXXXXXXXXX

XXXXXXXXXXXXX   XXXXXXXXXXXXX

XXXXXXXXXXXXX   XXXXXXXXXXXXX

So, now you both should have ten pairs, or twenty entries, one side with items or actions that remind you of your bad memory, and the other side with things you can do in the future to replace that bad memory with good. If you see shadows of demons floating around the person you love, just ignore them. Forget they're even there. Those demons aren't yours, and that's all that matters. Focus on your own demons now and learn to play this game.

4. To play, each of you will take turns reading an entry on your list, one at a time. You can read each entry in any order you choose. Just don't repeat the same entry twice. Mix them up. Make it as hard as you can for them. When the person you love reads an entry, write it down. They will do the same with yours.

5. Once you've both read your own and written down the other's twenty items, begin to guess which two on the other's list are pairs. Take turns, one guess per turn. When one of you is

correct, both of you will cross the pair off your lists.

6. The one who guesses all the pairs of items from the other's list first wins.

Don't let them win. Do everything you can to beat them. Play the best game you can. If you lose, let yourself be unhappy about it. If you win, rub it in. Then, talk about the things on each of your lists. Don't discuss the memories, only the fun ideas for the future.

Once the game is done and the topic is exhausted, do something around the house with the person you love. While you do, tell them about house sparrows, like me. Point to one outside your window and show them its egg-shaped body and brown-and-gray-and-white markings and little black smudges over the eyes like a mask so the person you love knows which bird you're talking about.

Tell them there's scarcely a place on Earth where humans live that house sparrows don't live with them and you'll never find a house sparrow out in the unsettled wild. In fact, entire colonies of sparrows can die if the humans they live around go away. Explain how the house sparrow outside the window got there by its ancestors flying across continents, stowing away on ships, and sometimes being intentionally carried by people across the world. And the ancestors of those house sparrows were there at the dawn of civilization as humans ground their first grains tens of thousands of years ago. House sparrows have seen rockets go into space. They were there as the pyramids of Egypt were built. They've been with humans since the very beginning.

Ask the person you love if they've ever imagined living tens of thousands of years ago, before civilization, and what they would've been good at. Think about that question as well and envision the person you would've been. Let part of yourself be a bird then too.

CPSIA information can be obtained
at www.ICGtesting.com
Printed in the USA
BVHW080924151122
651979BV00006B/165